Carved in Stone:
A Conversation With Our Ancestors

by William T. Everett

ISBN: 978-0-557-81825-9

Dedication

This book is dedicated to the memory of my ancestors
Those who lived and died on the continent of Africa
Those who survived and perished during the Middle Passage
Those who built these United States
hose who endured American slavery, emancipation, Jim Crow and the Civil Rights Movement

The memory of my father, Robert E. Everett, Sr.
To the memory of Deacon Kenneth "Uncle Kenny" Rolle

To my mentor and friend, Zolton "Lil Z" Holman
To my always supportive family & friends

Chapter One

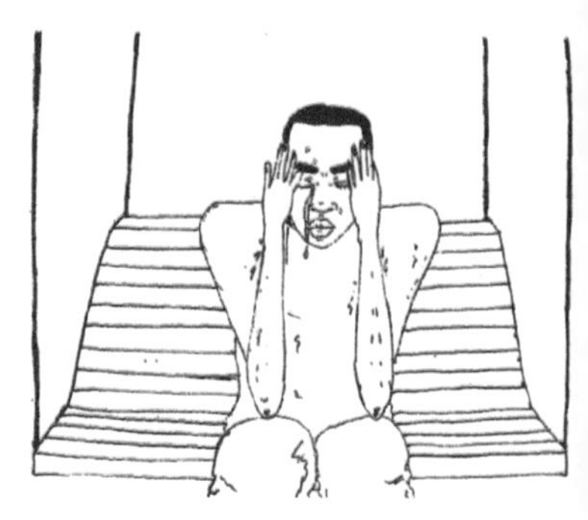

How can you love something—or someone—you've never seen yet hate your own reflection? Zolton, the owner of the darker complexion, wonders how...why? He got a few days to ponder at home alone. He promised himself that if they cracked one more 'you so black' joke that he was going to handle his business. They did - so did he. The principal did too by giving Zolton a three day home suspension.

He hates those boys for hating him and he's starting to hate himself, too. Maybe 'hate' is too strong a word but it sure feels like hate would—and should feel.

So caught up in his own thoughts, Zolton didn't notice that his uncle, Uncle Kenny, was in the house and had made his way back to the porch where Zolton was sitting.

Tall, handsome, and still pretty 'cut' for his age,

Uncle Kenny is no stranger to the taunts and verbal abuse of youth. For most of his life, he too endured countless put downs because he was darker than most. Uncle Kenny, however, found solace and strength in what he affectionately calls 'knowledge of self'.

"Hotep my young brother." announces Uncle Kenny as he walks up to Zolton.

"Hey Uncle Kenny," murmurs Zolton, head down, face still wrapped in his hands, only his lips and chin exposed.

"Young man, you look like you just lost your best friend. But more importantly, what are you doing home so early from school? It's only 1:30."

"Uncle K, the kids in school always make fun of me," his eyes still hidden, "and I just got tired of it."

"Why? What do they do? And what did *you* do?" asked Uncle Kenny, even though he already knew the entire story through Robin, his younger sister and Z's mother.

“They are always talking trash,” said Lil Z.

“Talk to me my brother. What types of ‘trash’?”

With a sharp turn of his head, his two blood-shot eyes caught his uncle’s squarely. Lil Z snaps, “They say, ‘**You so black we can’t see you at night - unless you smile**’ and crap like that. So I punched one of them fools in his face! I ain’t nobody’s punk.”

“Reeaally?” draws out Uncle Kenny. “How contradictory,” he says as he fights back the emotions of his childhood growing up in a segregated south. Wasn’t bad enough that the white folks hated the lil’ colored boy. No, he was even too dark for the ‘negroes’. Not too black to shoot that ball though. No, at six three, two forty, everyone wanted him to do *that*. Just too dark to have a promising future - ‘who’s gonna hire a darky like you?’ - and definitely too dark to play the lead role in the Negro school play. ‘We’ll let Jason have that role. He has the right ‘look’ ,’ said his 6th grade drama teacher. Never mind that a young Uncle Kenny ran circles around the fairer-skinned Jason during try outs. *How have our children—over a generation separated from segregation— inherited this emo-*

tional baggage?, Uncle Kenny now asks himself. *White folks water must still be wetter and their ice colder than black folks'.*

"Contradictory?" Lil Z asked interrupting Uncle Kenny's thought. "Are you using big words again?"

"Oh, sorry my brother," continues Uncle Kenny as he sits in the chair next to Z and gently places his hand on Z's shoulder. "Contradictory means inconsistent, logically opposite."

"Then why is it 'contradictory' that they make fun of me? I'm black, ain't I?" retorts Lil Z, his head rolling back down into his hands, elbows on his knees.

"Yes, you are black. But the contradiction—what is opposite- is that being 'dark' or 'black' is not a bad thing, it is a great thing."

"Yeah, right. You trippin' Uncle K." Z's eyes began welling up with tears, and his cheeks were flushed from pressing against the palms of his hands. “They make fun of all the really dark kids all the time. Light is good. Dark is bad. Nothing ‘opposite’ - contradictory—about that?” His gaze this time, remained steadfast, glaring at his uncle anxiously awaiting a response.

In the beginning “the earth was formless and empty, darkness was over the surface of the deep” thought Uncle Kenny. “*...the baby is formed in the darkness of it’s mother’s womb...the seed dies and is reborn in the darkness of mother earth…” Dark is bad? What could be further from the truth?*” “*Out of darkness comes the light...out of darkness comes life*”.

“Well?” says Lil Z, interrupting his thought.

“It’s a contradiction, my young brother,” Uncle Kenny said turning the chair to face Z, “because unlike today, thousands of years ago, people who were black like you ruled the civilized world. Our jet black African ancestors were kings, priests, scientists, doctors, engineers, artists, architects... We were not a minority in a great country, we were the majority who created one of the world’s first great civilizations.”

“Who? The slaves? They didn’t run nuthin’.” Zolton rolled his eyes to the back of his head in frustration.

“Not so fast my brother. Africans enslaved in America, the Caribbean and Brazil were organized and mounted slave revolts. And I know you’ve heard of the Underground Railroad led by Harriet Tubman. Also, small bands of Africans enslaved in Haiti, led by Toussaint L’Ouverture, ran off the mighty British and French armies. Our ancestors’ strength and courage is something that we all should be proud of.”

“Yeah, yeah - we shall overcoooome someday,” Lil Z sarcastically sings as he stands, placing his right hand over his heart and looking off into space.

“But I’m not talking about those black Africans,” continued Uncle Kenny, ignoring Z. “No, my brother. Always remember that black—African—history does not begin with the Transatlantic Slave Trade.”

“Why are you always talking about slavery? That’s over and done with. Move on old man.”

“You go to church every Sunday to be reminded about somebody else’s supposed slavery, but you want to forget about your own? Now that is a contradiction.”

“Maaa-muh,” yells Lil Z. “Uncle Kenny is talking bad about church again.”

“Kenneth,” a voice calls from inside the house. “You leave my baby alone.”

Uncle Kenny hears his sister’s footsteps coming down the hall as the voice approaches, “You hear me Kenneth James? You leave my baby alone.” Robin appears in the doorway.

“Aww, baby sistah, I was just teaching ‘yo baby’ the meaning of the word contradiction. That’s all.”

“Kenneth James, I know that tone. Don’t start with me.”

"Like the contradiction that you all can't even get in the car good after church on Sunday before he turns on that woman-hatin' nonsense called rap music? Contradiction." he said turning to look at Z.

"There you go Kenneth. I'm about to go the store. Keep it up and I'm taking Zolton with me and you'll be rantin' and ravin' to yourself."

"Or how about the contradiction," Kenny said looking at Robin, "That I can't discuss the horrors of American slavery and Jim Crow but he can spend hours mastering a video game where the black man steals cars, kills prostitutes and has deadly shoot outs with the police." Turning back to Z, "Contradiction, my lil' brother."

"You got one more time…", says Robin before being cut off.

Looking off into the distance Uncle Kenny continued "...and how ya'll goes to church every Sunday and learnz Jewish 'his-tory' and he goes to yo' school everyday to learnz American 'his-tory' but our own story is just 'the past' and we need to forget about it?" With a stern look at Lil Z, Uncle Kenny stated again, "Contradiction!"

"That's it!" as Z's mom grabbed his arm an pulled him up out of his chair towards the doorway. "We're out of here. Lock the bottom lock on your way out Kenneth. You need Jesus big brother."

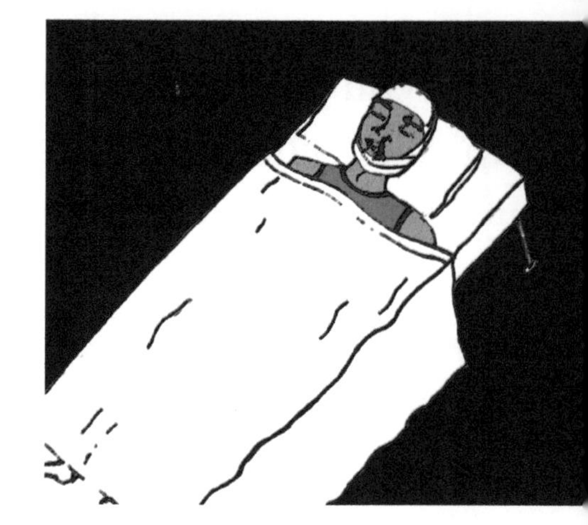

Actually, years ago he was hot and heavy over Jesus and the church - until that basketball incident. Not on the court, mind you, but off. Seems the town folk didn't take too kindly to the all-black team whoopin' up on the all-white team in the 'friendly scrimmage'. As he laid in the segregated hospital bed that night, bruised physically and mentally, a young Kenneth wondered, *What god would allow this to happen? Why are black folks always catching hell and then turning the other cheek?* He had no more cheeks to turn after that night.

"My dear baby sister Robin," Uncle Kenny said

as he grabbed Z's other arm. "Wait, wait. I'm sorry I got a little carried away. Go on to the store and I'll wait here with Z and I promise," he raised his right hand, "on a stack of bibles that I won't say anything directly or indirectly about your beloved church."

Lil Z, dangling between the two siblings, smirks. He loves it when these two go at it.

"Z," his mother says, staring in Uncle Kenny's eyes, "if he says one thing you get up and go lock yourself in your room until I get back." Turning to look at Z she continued, "You understand me?"

"Yes Ma'am."

Lil Z's mother quickly whispers to her older brother, " You are supposed to be here cheering him up not causing problems. Please big brother, encourage your nephew."

She then kisses Z and leaves the house.

Chapter Two

"So where was I?" starts Uncle Kenny, "Oh yeah our story. Slavery in America is just a small but important part of our *written* story that spans over 5,000 years. Before there was a Europe—black people—your ancestors in Ancient Kemet– created great civilizations that flourished for thousands of years."

"Chemist? What's an African chemist got to do with anything?", asked Z.

"Kem—et not Chem-ist. Kemet means 'black'. It is what your African ancestors called themselves and the land that provided for them."

"Uncle Kenny," replied Lil Z, "you don't have to tell me any fairy tales to make me feel better. I know how to handle it. If they get out of line again, I'll just roll up on those nig.."

"...Calm down my brother. Remember that 'emotions are good servants but poor masters'. Violence and name calling are not how an intelligent young man, such as yourself, resolves a conflict. Besides, you can't be mad with them. Those boys just don't know themselves."

"They just don't know what?" Lil Z responds raising his voice. "Well, I know 'em—I can tell you exactly who they are. Why are you makin' excuses for people? Man, that's why I can't stand black people."

"So you can't stand yourself now, huh?"

"I'm not black"

"Then what color are you?"

A dead silence.

"I'm...brown. Maybe purple. Yeah, call me 'purple man'."

"Ok 'purple man'. But why purple?"

" Anything but black 'cause if I was black—like them - they wouldn't make fun of me, now would they? How's that for logically consistent, my older brother?" Lil Z says sarcastically.

Unfortunately, it did make a lot of sense, thought Uncle Kenny. But he couldn't tell Z this. "Glad you asked the question. They wouldn't make fun of you if they knew themselves—the glorious accomplishments of our black African ancestors—people who looked just like you and them...us."

They don't know themselves? This old dude is trippin' cause all I know , thought Lil Z, *is that every year at the end of January they put up the same old posters and tell the same old stories about the same old people. Ain't nobody trying to hear that stuff. And sure nuf, when March 1st rolls around, it's back to the same ole same ole. All they really care about is passing that stupid state test. Know themselves*! *Yeah right*.

"Oh. Here ya go with one of those 'back-to-Africa-black-history' speeches again and it ain't even February." sings Lil Z as he stands throwing his hands in the air. "Uncle K, I'm not really feelin' that right now."

“No speech this time my brother. This time I’ll show you our greatness—carved in stone—in ancient Kemet. Let’s go back to Ancient Kemet right now!” thrusting his index finger down on the “right” and “now”.

“What da? Huh? You been burnin’ too many of those sticks of incense Uncle K. How are we going to Africa right now?” mimicking his uncle’s hand jesters.

At that very moment a portal to Kemet opened just a few feet away from where they are standing. As the portal opens, Uncle Kenny’s eyes widened...

“Ooooh yes, my brother,” announces Uncle Kenny. “Through this portal we’ll go back thousands of years to witness how our black ancestors, the Kemetnu, lived. It’s literally carved in stone. Get in.”

Chapter Three

"Wow, Uncle Kenny. This is tight. Where are we?"

"Glad you asked the question. We are in North Africa. Specifically, Ancient Kemet. Kemet is a part of Africa and don't let anybody tell you it's in the 'Middle East' or somewhere else."

"If you look at a map today Kemet is called 'Egypt'," continued Uncle Kenny.

"This particular place is the great temple complex at 'Ipet-isut', or 'The most sacred place'. Your ancestors called it 'Waset'. It is the worlds largest religious complex."

"Hey, didn't Martin Luther King, Jr. give a speech here?"

"No Lil Z," replied Uncle Kenny with a little chuckle, "You're thinking about the 1963 March on Washington at the Washington Monument in Washington, D.C. But *NOW* you see where they got the idea for the monument."

"So the new chemist .."

"...Kemetnu"

"Yeah, the chemist-new got this idea from George Washington?"

"Just the opposite my brother. The Americans and Europeans stole the idea from your black African ancestors."

"Why are you always accusing someone of *stealing* something?"

"What do they call it when you copy someone's paper, rewrite it a little bit, give it to your teacher and say it was yours without giving that person credit?"

"Plagiarism." said Lil Z.

"Correct! Well do an Internet search on 'Washington Monument' and 'reflecting pool' and see if they give your black African ancestors the credit they deserve. Is that not plagiarism?

"Well, I guess…"

"Don't guess my brother. You got to know yourself, for yourself. See that tall thing there?" Uncle Kenny asked pointing to the obelisk.

"Yes."

"The Kemetnu called it a 'tekhenu' meaning to

pierce the sky. The Greeks named it 'obeliskos' where we get our current term, obelisk. Once there were two here at this very spot. But, in 1829, a foreign invader, Mehet Ali, took the other tekhenu from this temple and gave it to the French. It is still in the Place de la Concorde in Paris, France."

"Wow. He moved one of those all the way to France? That thing is huge."

"I never said they were small time crooks! But get this, my Nubian brother, there are 21 known original Kemetic tekhenu in the world. But there are only 5 left in Kemet."

"Five left out of 21? That's a lot of er uh...*borrowing*. Where are they now?"

"All over the world, my brother. At least 8 are in Rome, Italy. Every last one of them with a Christian cross on top! Contradiction."

"Why is a cross on top of an obelisk a contradiction?"

"Well my brother, they claim your ancestors worshiped many gods."

“You mean they were polytheistic,”interjects Z.

“Exactly my brother but that was not true. *But*, even if the Romans *thought* your ancestors were polytheistic, why would they put the symbol of Christianity—the cross—on top of a supposedly polytheistic symbol?”

“Hmmm. Good question Uncle Kenny. That does sound a bit-illogical.”

“There is even a copy of a tekhenu right here in Texas and an original in New York’s Central Park. They say the copy near Houston—the San Jacinto monument— was the ‘brainchild of architect Alfred C. Finn, engineer Robert J. Cummins, and Jesse H. Jones’. Whattun no ‘brainchild’. It’s design was copied from your ancestors straight out of Kemet with no credit. Plagiarism!”

“Calm down Uncle Kenny, calm down. I get it. So the United States got the idea for the Washington Monument— tech-a-new — from black Africans in Ancient Kemet?

“Yes, sir. From your ancestors. You got to know

yourself, for yourself."

"I got a question for you Uncle K. Why did you leave the church? Mama said it was because you got beat up by some white people, and because of that, you couldn't play basketball anymore."

Ignoring Lil Z Uncle Kenny continues, "Do you know what they call the tekhenu that is in New York's Central Park?" asked Uncle Kenny.

"That's a contradiction Uncle Kenny."

"What is my brother?"

"You always tellin' me to 'ask the question' and now I'm asking and you won't answer. Contradiction?"

"Ouch! I guess you've got a point there my brother. Well, back when I was in high school, we had a basketball scrimmage—an all-black team versus an all-white team. There were no mixed teams back then. We skunked them boys pretty good that day. But later on, just as we were leaving the gym through the back door, a group of white boys came out of nowhere and started wailing on us. We didn't know what had hit us. I just remember waking up in a hospital bed, body aching from head to toe."

"As I laid in that hospital bed," Uncle Kenny continued almost in a whisper, eyes glazed over, "I had nothing but time to think. All I could do was wonder why—why me? Why us? - Why do black folks catch so much hell? Without me saying a word, the old man in the bed across from me—like he was reading my mind—started talking to me."

"Don't just ask the question young man. Go, search for the answers to those questions."

"What, old man? Do I know you?" I said indignantly.

"No, but I know what you're thinking. I've had those same questions. Saw a good friend lynched when I was 'bout your age. Jusfuh lookin' wrong at a white man. Didn't start looking at the ground fast enough I guess. Disrespectful, ya know. They could do that back when I was comin' up. Nowadays at least they gotta think twice 'bout killin' us."

“So that’s when you started reading all those books, Uncle K?”asked Lil Z.

“Yes my brother. The old man turned me on to ‘The Miseducation of the Negro’ by Dr. Carter G. Woodson and ‘Stolen Legacy’ by George G.M. James. As I got older I continued to read books like ‘African Origins of Western Religion’ by Dr. Ben Jochannan & ‘They Came Before Columbus: The African Presence in Ancient America’ by Dr. Ivan Van Sertima. I learned our story and not ...”

“...Who came before Columbus Uncle Kenny?”, interrupted Lil Z.

“Africans from Guinea, my brother. When Columbus arrived in the Americas the local people told him about your African ancestors that traded with them.”

“Are you serious Uncle Kenny?”

“Yes. They gave Columbus spear points made by your ancestors. Columbus took them back to Spain to be tested and sure ‘nuf, it has the same composition as the spear points from Guinea.”

“Wow Uncle Kenny. You REALLY began to know yourself, for yourself, huh?”

“Yes my brother. I couldn’t free my mind based on the old man’s knowledge. That was his knowledge. I had to read for myself, get my own knowledge. I made the time to learn our story for myself.”

“Soooo did you answer my question? Why did you leave the church?” asked Lil Z

“Don’t get me wrong my young brother. There are well meaning people in the church and I’m not sayin’ you should leave. Nevertheless, I’ve come to learn through all my years of study that they teach us only half the story.”

“Half? So what’s the other half?”

“Yes, half my brother, especially the Old Testament. For example, you’ve got to ask yourself, what was so special about Kemet—our ancestors’ land—that Abraham, Isaac, Joseph & Moses went there and lived there? Why does the black church only preach about their story and not teach about our African part of the story?”

"Not sure I follow you Unc."

"Go back and read the book of Genesis. Each time there was a famine somebody—Abraham and Joseph's brothers —travelled to Kemet. Even Jesus went to Kemet when King Herod was trying to kill him. Then ask yourself a few *more* questions my Nubian scholar. What is the other half of the story? What was so special about Kemet that it was such a safe place for so long? Why did our ancestors have food when everyone else was starving? Why did we have a great civilization - religion, monuments, philosophy, advanced agriculture - when everyone else was roaming around trying to find a place to call home? Why don't the preachers teach us that part—our ancestors' half of the story? Even Moses 'was educated in all the wisdom of the Egyptians and was powerful in speech and action' . Do you know that one time I asked the preacher 'what wisdom' they were referring to regarding Moses and dat preacher looked at me like I was crazy?"

"You got a point. I never thought of it that way," replied Z. "I always thought pharaoh was our enemy. You know, 'let my people go'. Never thought of him as one of us....our ancestors."

"And THAT is all I ever ask you to do."

"What's that Uncle Kenny?"

"I want you to become a man who thinks about what he believes rather than believe what he's never thought about. And that's with everything - Internet, magazines, television, newspapers, books, teachers - even question me."

"I get you. Ask the question, huh Uncle Kenny?"

"Exactly. Know yourself for *yourself.* You kids today have so much information at your finger tips. Don't just take someone else's word for it. Investigate! Consider! I mean, think critically about it on your own just for a minute. Pharoah - your African ancestor - as your enemy? What a contradiction! We don't know ourselves—our story—'cause we spend too much time learning and embracing his story. We spend too much time having conversations with their ancestors and not enough time in conversation with our own ancestors."

"Uncle Kenny" asks Z," how in the world do you conversate with an ancestor and that person is dead?"

"You read about them my brother because they speak to us through their stories. They share their wisdom and knowledge through books, recorded conversations and stories told by the living who knew them."

"Who do you talk to Uncle Kenny?"

"I talk to your grandfather, Robert."

"Uncle, that was one wild dude. What do you talk to him about?"

"He used to always tell me 'Son, stay focused. Keep your eyes forward like a race horse with blinders on. Don't look to the left. Don't look to the right. Keep looking at your goal."

"So", continued Uncle Kenny, "When I pray I remember our conversations and I ask him to help keep me focused. To help me live the life he wanted for me."

"That's deep Uncle Kenny. Coversations with dead people."

“That’s right my brother. We got to talk to ‘em to know our story, not just ‘his story’.”

“Dats cool, dats cool Uncle Kenny”, said Lil Z. “But what’s up with all this ‘his story’ and ‘our story’ stuff? History is history, isn’t it?”

“Not exactly my brother,” said Uncle Kenny. “Depends on who’s writing the story. Our *written history* is over 5000 years old. You see it now here in Kemet. It’s carved in stone! But your ‘his story’ book would lead you to believe that ‘our story’ is only 500 years old starting with the first African slave arriving here in 1502. And just this past year they went and rewrote the ‘his story’ books in your great state of Texas.”

“What do you mean Uncle Kenny?” asked Z.

“Boy don’t you read the paper? A small group of folks went and changed the Texas ‘his story’ curriculum to reflect what they thought was right. You bettah ask somebody!”

“Uncle Kenny, Mama says you hate white people. Is that true?”

"Not at all," said Uncle Kenny calmly. "Just because I love black folks— people of African descent —doesn't mean I hate white folks. What I hate are the lies that have been and continue to be told to us. And it doesn't matter the color of the person telling the lie either."

"You know Uncle K, you're not as crazy as I thought you were. So what else did we get from Kemet?"

" You're learning. You *got* to ask the question! But your mom will be back from the store real soon. We gotta get back to the house."

"Come on Uncle Kenny, one more thing about my 'black African ancestors'. You want me to know myself, don't you?" says Lil Z with a wry smile.

"Niiiice. You know I can't say no to that. What they stole my Nubian Prince is literally carved in stone. But I can show you better than I can tell you."

The portal appears again.
"Let's bounce!"says Uncle Kenny.

Chapter Four

“Oooh, Uncle Kenny! I know what these are.”

“ What my brother?”

“ These are the buildings the Hebrew slaves built

when the king—the dude with the pony tail—wouldn't give them straw. Moses told him, 'let my people go'. I see it on TV every year around Easter."

"That my brother is what your grandmother would call a 'bald faced lie'. That movie is his story, not your story. These are the Great Pyramids at Giza. The large one in the middle– the Great Pyramid of Khufu—was built over 4,000 years ago with an estimated 2,300,000 stone blocks.

Each block weighed an average of 2.5 tons each. The blocks were cut from quarries in Aswan—500 miles away—by skilled masons."

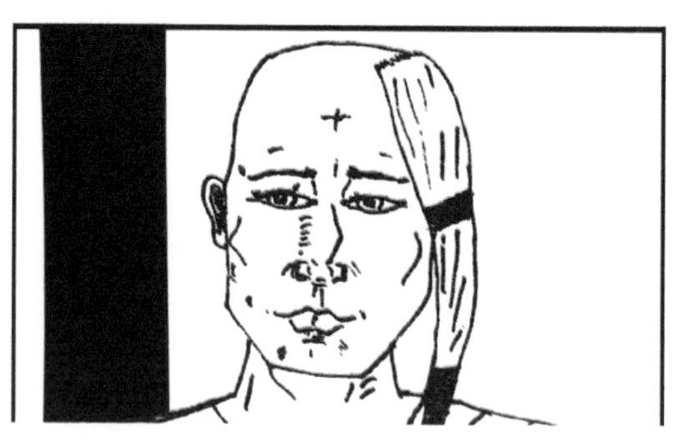

"Really! 4000 years ago, huh? Straw buildings don't last that long do they?"

"No sir. And no Hebrew slaves built it either my Lil brother. You had to be a master builder to work on these pyramids. Did you know that Khufu's pyramid —built by your African ancestors—was the tallest man-made structure in the world for over 3,800 years?"

"Thirty-eight hundred! That's over...2010 minus 1776 - plus 4 - 80 - plus 30 - 234. That building is over 15 times as old as the United States!"

"Yes sir and that is only one of many magnificent structures built by your ancestors."

"Black Africans have been around that long?" asked Z.

"Much longer. You remember Abraham and Moses in the Bible?"

"Of course. I just told you Moses freed the Jews from the Egyptian... I mean the chemist-new Pharaoh."

“I’ll let that comment slide for now. Anyway my brother, the mother of Abraham’s first son—Ishmael—was an African woman named Hagar. And Moses’ wife was a black African, too.”

“You know now that you mention it, didn’t Moses’ brother, Aaron, diss Moses for marrying an African woman?”

“You got to know it! But do you remember seeing an African wife in that movie of yours, ‘The Ten Commandments’? No siiir you didn’t! His story, not our story.”

“How do you know she was black?”, asked Lil Z.

“Ha ha glad you asked the question. The name ‘Ethiopia’ comes from the Greek word ‘Aethiopia’ which means ‘Land of the Burnt Face’. Same as the word ‘Cush’ in the bible.”

“Guess you can’t get much blacker than ‘burnt face’ huh?”, asked Lil Z with a proud smile.

“You got to know it!”, shouted Uncle Kenny. “So next time those boys make fun of you, tell ‘em you‘re not just black, you're a ‘burnt face' brother."

"But, hold on my brother," continued Uncle Kenny. "We go back a lot further than those bible stories. Both of the oldest known relatives of ALL mankind were found in the land of burnt face, just south of Kemet. Ever heard of Ardi and Dingnesh?"

"Ardi yes but the other ‘D' one, no."

"Well the people that found Dingnesh in Ethiopia called her ‘Lucy' after an old Beatles song. They just luv givin' us names—'Lucy', 'endangered', ‘at-risk'.... Anyway, Dingnesh is what the Ethiopians call her."

"Is that why Africa is called the ‘Cradle of Civilization' Uncle Kenny?"

"My brother, my brother you're beginning to see the light! Keep on asking the question and you'll get your answer."

"Knowledge is power, huh Uncle Kenny?"

“No my brother. Knowledge by itself is just...well knowledge. Using knowledge to get what you want and need is power. I know a lot of folks with plenty of knowledge and no power.”

“Man you got an answer for everything”, replied Z . “Anyway, so next I guess you’re gonna tell me they stole the pyramids too?”

“Let me hold a dollar,” said Uncle Kenny.

“Right now?” asked Lil Z as he reached into his pocket.“I don’t see any stores around here but if that’s what you want. Here ya go.”

“You see that?” pointing to the pyramid on the back of the dollar.

“ Whoooooaaa! I never noticed that pyramid on the back.”

“The truth is often hidden in plain sight. Your ancestors’ pyramid is part of the ‘Great Seal—Reverse’ on the US dollar. But that’s not it. Look to the right of the ‘reverse’. That’s called the ‘Great

Seal—Obverse'. Guess where they got THAT from?"

"Well let me guess. Uhh, Kemet?", says Z sarcastically.

"You got jokes my brother but yes, Kemet. It was copied from your ancestors' Emblem of Heru. I mean count the number of arrows...look at the sun over the head."

"My goodness! We got Kemet everywhere in the United States. Created by folks as dark as me?"

"Yes my brother. And we haven't even scratched the surface. You still 'can't stand' black folks?"

1 ONE
1 ONE
ONE
1 ONE
1 ONE

Chapter Five

"What's wrong Z?" Uncle Kenny asked. "You got quiet on me."

" Nuthin', " replied Z as he stared down at his feet.

"I know you better than that my brother. What's up?"

Turning his head back toward his uncle, Z asked, "Uncle Kenny, what does third world country mean?"

"Why do you ask that?"

"Well, in my geography book, they talk about countries in Africa as third world countries. Then, I see all these things on TV with little black kids with big stomachs and flies flyin' all around them. Mamma says their stomachs are big 'cause they are starving."

"Ok", said Uncle Kenny.

"Then I see stuff about Africans at war," continued Z. "Small boys like me with guns. Then you see another story where African people have AIDS and stuff. Dying all over the place. Now you come telling me that my African ancestors did all this great stuff."

"It's carved in stone, my brother. What's on your mind?"

"My point is, if Africa is so bad, why did the Americans and Europeans steal so much stuff from Africa and not tell anybody? Why don't they teach us about the black Africans from Kemet in history class? All they ever talk about is *overcomin'* this and *sufferin'* through that."

"Uh huh my brother," replied Uncle Kenny with a warm smile, "Now you are beginning to know yourself, for yourself! Now you see what I mean by contradiction or opposite as you say."

"Not again Uncle Kenny,"said Z with frustraton, "I'm serious Uncle Kenny! Please, for once just answer the question. Why don't we learn about this in school?"

"Z, you ever hear the story about the eagle that grew up as a chicken?" asked Uncle Kenny.

"Sounds familiar but what does that have to do with anything? Are you going off on a tangle again?"

"You mean *tangent*," Uncle Kenny exlained. "No, I'm not going off on a tangent. Just work wit' me for a minute. Remember the eagle egg got mixed up with the chicken eggs. So when the eagle egg hatched with all the chicken eggs…"

"... yeah, yeah," interupted Z, "The eagle thought the chicken was his mother and that he was a chicken."

"Riiiight when in fact, he really was an eagle.

What else happened?"

"Well, he grew up acting like a chicken – cluckin' eating feed off the ground – even tried to crow like a rooster a couple of mornings."

"Uh huh. And how did he feel living with those chickens?" Uncle Kenny asked anxiously.

"He felt a lil'…I mean a lot out of place. He didn't look like them. He knew something was different about him and he kept looking up in the sky and dreamin' about flying and stuff."

"Yep." added Uncle Kenny, "But the other chickens told him he couldn't do it 'cause he was just a chicken and chickens don't fly. Until one day…"

"… Until one day another eagle noticed him and swooped down to holler at him." continued Z. "He asked him why he was hanging out with chickens and not flying like the

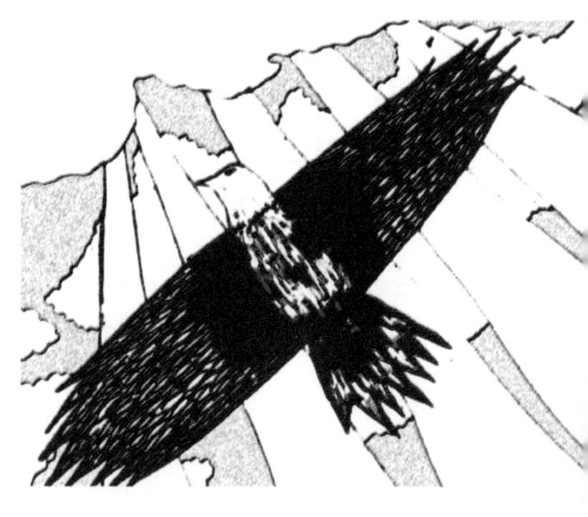

rest of the eagles."

"Then..."

"Then the chicken-eagle said, 'I ain't no eagle, I'm a chicken' ," continued Z. "But the more he looked at the other eagle, the more he realized that he WAS an eagle and not a chicken. He began to know himself, for himself. And he began to..."

"... fly like the rest of the eagles!" Uncle Kenny exclaimed. "And that is why, my brother, they hide your story from you. Because if you knew that you were the originators not the imitators – the teacher and not the student - then you would have the courage to fly like the mighty and majestic eagle that you are. But instead, you don't know your ancestors—the great shoulders upon which you stand. So you run around like a 'chicken-eagle' – pants saggin', denying and ashamed of your true self. Talkin' 'bout light-skinned is better than dark-skinned. Calling yourself African American but don't want nuhthin' to do wit' no Africa. Spendin' all your vacation money in Europe and Mexico."

"You see this?", continued Uncle Kenny, pointing. “Notice anything strange about it?”

“Yes. The nose is broken off the Sphinx,” replied Z proudly. “ I see that in a lot of the pictures from Kemet.”

“You mean Horem Akhet. Sphinx is a foreign name. NEVER let anyone give you a name my brother. But anyway, for years, the Europeans, especially the Greeks—Thales of Miletus, Pythagoras and Anaximander just to name a few- studied in ancient Kemet. But when foreigners finally took over Kemet in 332 B.C.E., they tried to destroy,

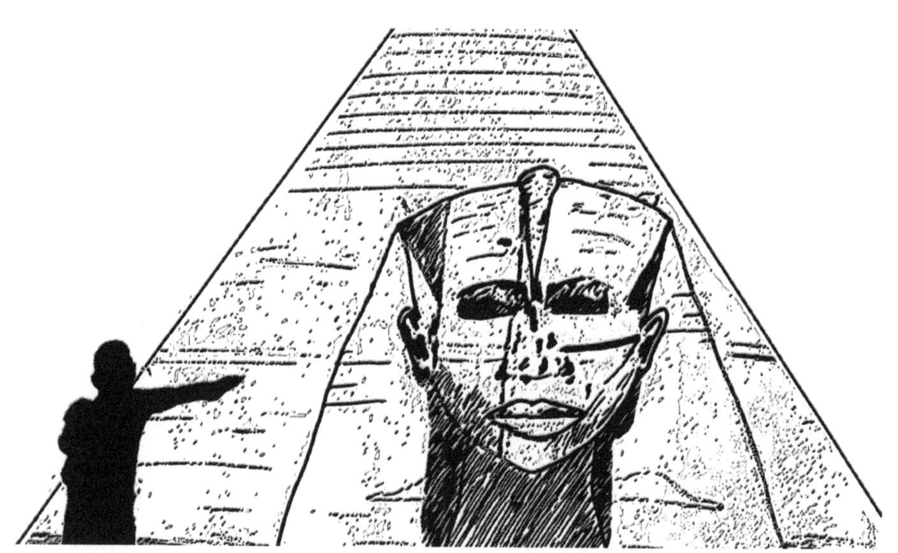

distort or hide all that was black, even down to your broad, distinctly black noses.”

“Z”, continued Uncle Kenny, “they don’t teach you about your greatness because they want to claim all they can as their own. They want you to believe that you’ve given the world nothing and that they have created or founded just about everything. They want you to hate Africa and believe that your history began with slavery.”

“But in reality,” said Lil Z as he grazed his hand across the cool stones. “My ancestors created a lot of stuff. I mean, its carved in stone.”

“Yes, it is. So now that you know what they don’t teach you and why they don’t teach it, you also understand why we cannot expect anyone else to teach us our true history. We have to go get it ourselves. We’ve got to ask the question...We’ve got to - ”

“... know ourselves, for ourselves, huh?” interrupted Lil Z, eyes bright, still caressing the monument. “No more “chicken-eagles!”

“That’s right. No more chicken-eagles. You GOT tah know it!”

"But you know what else I've noticed Uncle Kenny?"

" What's that Z?"

"I've noticed that even when they talk about Kemet, no one really talks about the color of the chemist new. Sometimes when you're reading or watching the shows, it's like they have no color or they say it doesn't matter what color they are."

"Until the lion has a story teller, the hunter will always have the best part of the story," said Uncle Kenny.

"Oh lawd! First chickens, then eagles and now lions needin' to hire a story teller."

"Until we go back and learn—and tell—our own story," explained Uncle Kenny, as he turned to point to the many monuments surrounding them. "The hunter will always tell the story the way he wants it told. *His story.* Let me give you another example my brother. Ever see the movie, 'The Mummy'?"

"Yeah...I mean yes sir."

“Well, the name of the evil spirit is Imhotep, right?”

“I think so. Why?”

“Well, that is the hunter’s version of the story. The lion’s version —our story—is that your African ancestor Imhotep was a great scholar, physician, philosopher & builder. However, the hunter has once again contradicted our story, misrepresenting your ancestor as an evil spirit to be destroyed by the hunter.”

“Ok, ok. I got it. So we don’t learn about this—our story—in school because the ‘*hunter*’ doesn’t want us to know it. And because we don’t know it—our story— we don’t know who we are? And because we don’t know who we are, we don’t like ourselves?”

“Z, what does ‘poverty’ mean?” asked Uncle K.

“It means you’re broke. No dinero. Why do you always answer a question with another question?”

“Yes, poverty means that. But it also means that you don’t have- you lack - something that you need. It doesn't always mean money."

"So they insult me because they don't have any money? Because they are broke chicken-eagle li-ons with no story teller? You're making my head hurt Uncle K."

"No, black is not an insult because you don't have money. Those boys THINK black is an insult be-cause they lack—are 'poor' in - the knowledge of themselves. In the book of Thomas, Jesus of Nazareth said,

> '*When you come to know yourselves, then you will become known, and you will real-ize that it is you who are the sons of the living father. But if you will not know your-selves, you dwell in poverty and it is you who are that poverty.*'

"You see, those boys can't appreciate how great they— we are, because they don't know them-selves. They don't know themselves because they don't know their true story. "

"So if they—we—know the truth about ourselves", said Z, "—our real story—then we won't think being black is a bad thing?"

" Correct!", said Uncle Kenny, "When you know that you have greatness in you, then you will do great things. When you know the truth—that your ancestors have done great things -then you know that you can do even greater things. That's why I wasn't trippin' about Obama becoming president."

"You know I remember that about you. Why was that?" asked Z.

"Well my brother the way I see it Obama becoming President of the United States was just our story repeating itself."

"What?", asked Z.

"It was our story repeating itself.", said Uncle Kenny. "A man of African descent in charge of the most powerful country in the world."

"Well", started Z, "I guess if you look at it from that-"

"...Point of reference", interrupted Uncle Kenny.

"Yeah, that point of reference. That's deep Uncle Kenny. I guess knowing where you're going car really depend on knowing where you've been Going from *Pharoah* to president is a lot differen than *slave* to president."

"Just the ebb and flow of *our story* my brother" says Uncle Kenny, "but if all you know is *his story* - the lies, the contradictions-"

"...then you won't know the whole truth about being a burnt face. And you end up tearing down what you should be liftin' up." interrupted Z.

"The truth is beginning to set you free, my lil' brother. The truth is setting you free."

"Uncle K, I never heard of a Book of Thomas. There is no Book of Thomas, is it?"

"Is that a question or a statement my brother?"

"OMG! There you go again Uncle Kenny. Let's go home. *This* burnt-faced lion needs to go and learn OUR story."

"Hotep my brother. Hotep."

Please visit our online, interactive bibliography @
www.carvedinstone-thebook.com

www.ingramcontent.com/pod-product-compliance
Ingram Content Group UK Ltd.
Pitfield, Milton Keynes, MK11 3LW, UK
UKHW041839200726
13854UKWH00003BA/1214

9 780557 818259